CW00351093

1

Book 3

It's been a while since I wrote a book about heat pumps. Nothing massive has really changed in the last year or so. The kit has got bicker, quieter and hotter. Its not cheaper though.

The take up of the technology has been woeful in the UK, I think mostly due to us "heat pump experts" making it more complex than it needs to be combined with the British aversion to any change.

You can have a heat pump if you want one, you don't have to have one if you are not a fan you are not breaking the law if you buy or run a boiler.

Heat pumps do work. There is nothing magic about them, they are just boilers that live in the garden.

Graham Hendra the Scottish Highlands October 2023.

I hope this book helps answer a few questions you might have. If not try book 1 and 2

Thanks for buying it., if you stole it, fair play.

Contents:

32) When I have a shower warm water goes down the drain, can I recycle this heat?
33) Can I trust the heat meter readings in my heat pump controller?
34) How and why does my heating cost alter over the year? Or why is my run cost so high in Winter?
35) What is freeze up prevention and how does it work?
36) WRAS heat pumps and hot water only solutions
37) Can I heat my house and my swimming pool with the same heat pump?
38) Can I run my heat pump to work with my variable / flexible electricity tariff?
39) Should I have a smart meter if I want renewables at home?
40) Will the grid cope if we all go heat pump?
41) Why are there so many types of heat pump?
42) I keep seeing incredible COP figures online, should I trust them and what the theoretical maximum?
43) How should I look after my heat pump? ACF50
44) What's the best compressor in a heat pump?
45) Modulation and inverters? What does that mean?
46) Recirculation pumps
47) Are heat pumps noisy, an update.
48) How does a heat pump work?
49) Why your heat pump weather comp is set to 37 degrees, The Lizzie curve.
50) How long do heat pumps last?

1 Do I need planning permission for a heat pump?

For some completely unfathomable reason you need planning permission for a heat pump. To get planning permission there are two options:

The first is apply for planning to the local authority, never a fun time and not quick.

The second is do the MCS paperwork. There is a clause in MCS that says if the heat pump is installed and signed off for MCS then you can fit it with no planning permission under a scheme called permitted development. To get MCS sign off there are a few rules you must meet with reference noise but these days with quiet units they are a formality.

Permitted development was designed to let you make small changes to your house without needing any planning permission. For example, putting up a shed, garage, or conservatory.

So, the evil bit is even though you are not getting a grant you must pay someone like me to do all the paperwork for the system just so you can install it without planning. It's truly horrible and a total waste of time and money.

There is one other rule, the heat pump can't be installed within a metre of the boundary of the property, so you can't put it up against a fence.

Its madness but that's life.

2 Why can't I get a grant if I want to keep my boiler?

In the UK if you want to install a heat pump you have to fill in lots of paperwork. The main reason being that you can get £7500 towards your installation using the boiler upgrade scheme voucher. I guess no one wants to be held responsible for giving away government money without a procedure.

Our procedure is called MCS, its horribly flawed and ridiculously long, at last count it was 68 pages of forms to fill in. But you get £7.5 grand, so we soldier on without moaning and pass the cost to the homeowner.

But there is a problem, you only get the grant if you remove a fossil fuel boiler and replace it with a heat pump. If the boiler stays in there is no voucher.

Up until 2 years ago we used to let people put in a heat pump in tandem with their old boiler so the consumer could try it out and get familiar with it before going full renewable. It also helped for people with small power supplies or big houses. We called these systems hybrids.

If you install a hybrid there is no grant, you are on your own. And you must apply for planning permission.

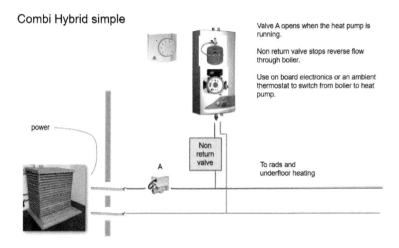

Combi Hybrid simple

Valve A opens when the heat pump is running.

Non return valve stops reverse flow through boiler.

Use on board electronics or an ambient thermostat to switch from boiler to heat pump.

power

Non return valve

A

To rads and underfloor heating

3 How can I tell if my heat pump isn't / is working well?

In cold weather we get reports that units are freezing up excessively or the unit is not achieving high enough radiator and floor temperatures:

This can be caused by the unit having a fault or it not being big enough for the job.

Firstly, we will test if the unit is working ok:

First draw off 30 liters of water from the cylinder, run a couple of taps for 5 mins to achieve this.

The heat pump should be able to achieve a 50C flow temperature without if it's working ok. If it's struggling to reach the 50C and it takes the hot water tank much longer to heat up than normal, you need an engineer.

If the unit can meet the tank temperature the heat pump is ok. Now we must make some more tests.

If its struggling to heat the house do some tests:

It's possible your unit is not set up to run warm enough, get your engineer to confirm the settings, you tube can help here, look for weather compensation settings.

But if your settings are ok and the radiators just never get warm enough, we need to prove the unit is big enough. We need to try to heat only ½ the house, to do this shut off half the radiators or half the underfloor heating first. Now let the unit run. If the radiator temperatures get much better / hotter the unit works but it just can't heat the whole house. Its time to call your installer and get them to need to get out your heat loss calculation and check it's been done correctly.

4 What is weather compensation?

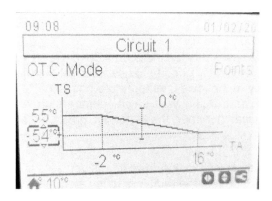

On ALL heat pumps the efficiency is highest when the water temperature is low, the efficiency falls as the temperature of the water increases. Setting the run temperature as low as possible gave the best efficiencies and therefore lowest run costs and biggest savings.

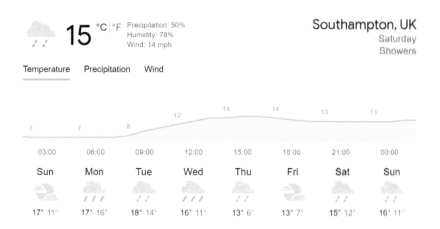

In most old heating systems, they work by pushing very hot water around whenever the boiler is on, typically you might see a radiator temperature of 70 degrees C. But a while ago someone clever worked out that you don't have to have the radiators red hot all the time. We could change the temperature of the radiators in line with the temperature outside.

When it's very cold outside the radiators would be 70 degrees C but as it got milder, we could allow the temperature of the radiators to fall. This was done to stop the radiators getting very hot, the room warming up too quickly then the boiler switching off again. This process is called weather compensation. basically, linking the radiator temperature to the outdoor temperature.

Every heat pump uses this technology as does every modern boiler. In heat pumps its especially good because we want to try and run the heat pump constantly at the lowest temperature possible. Remember you pay for the temperature, I always say the temperature of the radiators should be like miles per hour, the faster you go (or the hotter you go) the more it costs.

But.................. there is a major downside. If you set the weather comp up for efficiency and feel the radiators today at 5pm they could be running as low as 30 degrees C, it's enough to keep the house warm but the rads feel dead. As it gets colder outside the radiator temperature goes up and suddenly at about 37C they feel like they are working. At no point does the house go cold but people expect radiators to feel like they are on.

So, when I set up weather compensators, I don't set them to the most efficient setting, I always factor in comfort. I set them to have a minimum temperature of 37 degrees C when its 15 degrees C outside. This is when most heating in old houses starts up. I then let the radiators rise in temperature to 50 degrees C for low temp systems and 60C for high temperature using old radiators when its -2 degrees C outside.

If I wanted to get the most efficient setup, I would set the radiators to operate between 25C when its 15C outside up to 50C when its -2 C outside, but I don't, it's a delicate balance between efficiency and people moaning the rads are cold. If I did this the radiators would not reach 37 degrees C until it was well below 10 degrees outside, and I would get complaints the rads were cold. I know this because every time I do this at home that's exactly what happens.

Ok let's now get geeky. In some of the better heat pumps the manufacturers put a second level of weather compensation into the machine. This allowed the unit to firstly control using the outdoor temperature as described above but also monitor the indoor temperature. So, the unit would run on the external weather compensation figures to begin with but once it got close to room temperature the unit would tweak the water temperature to try and hold the rooms at the temperature you asked for.

The problem with it is you only have one controller measuring the temperature in one room, so everything hinges around where the controller was installed. If you put it in a cold or a hot room the weather compensation went wrong.

And now to get super geeky. If you wanted weather comp to be perfect, it would need to measure how humid it was outside and how much sunshine there was. It could then adjust the radiator temperature to include for solar gain. It could also predict how hot to run the rads based on previous experience and predicted weather. This was quite common in building management systems, but they use much more powerful chips and processors than what is found in the average domestic heating system.

This sort of functionality is now common if you install Homely and other bolt on heat pump controllers.

5 Is R290 dangerous and why use it?

R290 is the new buzzy refrigerant everybody is using in heat pumps. You will be familiar with R290, it's the gas you use in your barbeque, its Propane.

It's a cheap, low global warming potential refrigerant which happens to offer very high-water temperatures. R290 heat pumps can heat water to 80C, hotter than a boiler even when it's snowing outside.

The problem is it burns. All refrigerants have one bad characteristic.

In heat pumps you would typically have about 1kg or 1000g of R290, all of which is sealed inside the unit in the garden. If in the very unlikely event it leaked it would leak outside into the air. None of the refrigerant goes inside the house.

There are a lot of scare stories about this refrigerant but think about this, your deodorant can (and most other pressurised spray cans) is highly likely to use R290 as its propellant, the stuff that pressurises the can. You probably have a BBQ gas bottle in the shed or on the patio.

R290 is not new and if you don't set fire to your heat pump its safe.

If it scares you best put all those aerosols outside sharpish.

6 What qualifications do I need to install a heat pump?

Strictly speaking if you want to install a heat pump you don't need any qualifications at all. You could install it yourself as a diyer, but you won't get the grant.

The electrical part of the work is covered by the electrical regs, so you need to be a qualified electrician, but the plumbing is not.

BUT

If you want to get the BUS grant you have to be MCS accredited. To be MCS accredited you need a qualified plumber who has a heat pump qualification on top. Most plumbers can access this sort of course from BPEC and others in a 5-day course.

To install a pressurised hot water cylinder, you also need WRAS training and Unvented cylinder qualifications, these take a day to complete.

Heat pump designers often also have the low temperature heating design qualification too.

7 Can I use a heat pump to replace a big boiler in a commercial building? Churches etc?

Yes. Large heat pumps are available in low and high temperature options for commercial boiler replacement.

Its not quite as simple as swap the boiler for a heat pump. There are a few considerations:

A 1000kW boiler is the size of a very small car, a 1000kW heat pump is the size of an articulated lorry.

Boilers will probably already have a big gas supply. The heat pump will need a big electrical supply. This is the first consideration. Can you get a big electrical power supply in for a reasonable amount of money. If you can then the swap from gas to heat pump is simple.

8 What is an air-to-air heat pump and is it better?

Nobody calls air to air heat pumps, air to air heat pumps. We call them air conditioning units.

An air conditioning unit, like the one you have in your office or in your favourite shop is a heat pump. It does not heat water it heats air.

Every hotel you ever stay in is heated by nothing other than an air-to-air heat pump or air conditioning unit.

Are they better than air to water? Yes, in pretty much every way.

They are much cheaper to buy, you can have an air-to-air heat pump installed in your house for under £1000 foe one room.

They are much more efficient; in air-to-air systems you directly heat the air that blows into the room. The air only needs to be heated to about 40 degrees C. This is much easier and cheaper to do than heating water up to 50 or more degrees C to and pump it around radiators. So, air to air is cheaper to run,

It also cools, hey air conditioning cools shocker.

SO apart from being cheaper, more efficient and offer cooling why don't we sue them in the UK.

We in the UK like a radiator, in the far East houses are heated with air-to-air systems in almost all cases. No one uses radiators.

Our entire heating industry is based on people running pipes round houses to lumps of metal on the walls. It's a big jump to rip all that out and put in air conditioning. SO, we stick with the inferior technology.

9 Can I run an air-to-air heat pump off solar panels in cooling?

If you think about air conditioning in your car, when do you use it? in Summer when its sunny.

If you could hitch the air conditioning up to solar panels you could run it off the free electricity you are producing. Pretty tricky in a car but very easy in an office or a house.

It would be very easy to work out that you could produce electricity from your solar panels at home and use it to directly run the air conditioning system on a sunny day. The total CO_2 produced could be zero.

Solar PV and air conditioning in cooling are a near perfect match.

10 Why has solar PV taken over from solar thermal?

Solar thermal systems were very popular in the early 2000s but not so much now. Solar thermal is where you have panels with tubes on them up on the roof, running through the tubes is water. The sun heats the water which is pumped into the house. This technology was used to heat hot water cylinders and swimming pools and was very effective.

Its only problem was that once the hot water cylinder was hot and the pool up to temperature you couldn't do anything with the hot water you were making.

In solar PV the sun shines on the PV panels and makes electricity. You can use the electricity for whatever you like. The output from solar PV is much more useful, charge your car, fill up your batteries for later, heat your hot water or even sell the spare electricity back to your electricity supplier.

Solar Pv has become more common because its cheaper and more versatile than solar thermal. That's it. both works brilliantly. One has replaced the other.

11 What is an open system and are they "that good"?

There is a lot of talk on forums about open heating systems.

In most houses with a boiler, you have radiators with valves on where you can adjust the radiator output in each room to any temperature you like, these valves are called thermostatic radiator valves or TRVS. If they are set up well, they can work very well. In most cases they are not set up very well.

In an open system you don't have any valves. The system is balanced and set up to run in optimum conditions. The idea being that the water flows through all the rooms all the time (in heating season) to maintain every room just right. Before the advent of TRVs all systems were open.

Setting up an open system takes a bit more care but is not very hard.

The advantage of the open system is you can run the radiators longer but at a lower temperature, so the house maintains a flat even temperature all the time. It is the best and cheapest way to run a heat pump system. A good open system can save 30% of the run cost compared to a badly set up system with TRVs.

The only drawback to open systems is you can't or should not shut off rooms or run them colder than others, adjusting the system reduces its efficiency. And the radiators are much colder. The rooms are lovely and warm but when you touch the radiators, they don't feel hot.

So, if you want optimum efficiency, big carbon and run cost savings open is good. If you like warm rads less so.

12 What is a volumiser?

It has become very fashionable to use volumisers in heat pump systems.

A volumiser is just an insulated tank of water placed in the heating circuit. It looks like a 50-litre hot water cylinder.

A volumizer is installed in the heating circuit pipework, either on the way out to the radiators or on the way back, its aim is to add to the water volume of the system. Because the heat pump must heat up the volumizer as well as the radiators its like a small store of heat. The idea is this small store will stop the heat pump switching on and off so much, we call this cycling.

They are most effective in warmer weather when the heating load is small, and the heat pump tends to cycle like mad.

A volumizer is identical to a buffer vessel, its another name for the same thing.

The problem with them is they are expensive, they are big so where do you put this 50-litre hot water tank? and they slow down the heating circuit, so when you turn on the heating it lengthens the time to get the radiators warm.

With decent capacity control using inverter driven compressors they are not required. But some people like them, some manufacturers insist on them, so they linger on in our systems. I loathe them. They encourage poor system design and poor heat pump controls.

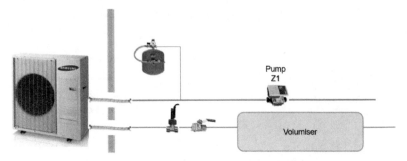

13 If I want to heat a conservatory with an air-to-air heat pump how do I know what size I need?

Sizing an air conditioning unit is simpler than sizing a heating system, the reason being we size for cooling not heating. The heating load of a room is always bigger than the heating load because we must cool the room down and fight the sunshine, any electrical loads, people, cats, dogs etc, all of which are basically just little heaters.

In heating systems, the sun, cats, dogs, electrical loads, and people all help us heat the room.

In large commercial systems it's a good idea to do a cooling load calculation but this is not necessary in a conservatory.

In a conservatory its normal to size the system purely on floor area. Measure the floor area in m^2. It's just length x width and multiply by 125 Watts for every metre square.

So, if your conservatory is 5 m x 4 m its 20 m^2. That means we need 20 x 125Watts or 2500 Watts. 2500 Watts is 2kW. Go for the next size up and you will be ok.

In this case a 3kW air to air heat pump is perfect.

14 How much heat can I get out of Under floor heating? Will it work in an old house?

Underfloor heating is very popular in modern houses. Instead of radiators a plastic pipe is run under the flooring to heat the room.

There are two factors effecting how much heat the UFH (as its known) can emit.

1 How hot the pipe is and how much pipe we can squeeze under the floor. The problem is you can't run very high (radiator) temperatures under the floor, if you did the floor would be too hot to stand on.

2 The amount of tube you can put in the floor is limited too. In the picture you can see the tubes are separated by a distance. We call, this the distance between centres. The closest you can run the tubes is 100mm apart, any closer and the pipes kink on the bends.

In new build, well insulated houses the tubes can be as much as 250mm apart because well insulated rooms need less heat.

set temp	250 centres	200 centres	150 centres	100 centres
35	57	62	73	78
40	78	84	91	98
45	108	117	128	137

The table above shows how much heat we can squeeze out of underfloor heating based on the set temperature we run the heat pump at and how close the tubes are together.

Example if you live in a badly insulated house with a heat loss of 100W / m^2 you would need either a 45C set temperature and 250mm centres or 40C set temperature and 100mm centres.

A new build house has a heat loss typically of 35W/m^2 see if you can work out the UFH for this house.

15 What is an average consumer? When the government talk about this person what do they look like?

When the government and the news talk about energy prices they keep referring to the average consumer and the average house without telling you who or what this is.

So, after a lot of work, I've managed to find out, here goes.

The average house is this one. They will pay £1923 a year for

From 1 October:

- The cost of electricity will fall from **30.1p per kWh to 27.35p**

- The price of gas will fall from **7.5p per kilowatt hour (kWh) to 6.89p**

This is based on an estimate that the average household uses 2,900 kWh of electricity and 12,000 kWh of gas.

And as for standing charges:

- They will be **53.37p per day** for electricity

- And **29.62p per day** for gas

gas and electricity.

The maths works like this:

There are 365 days a year, the standing charge is £0.5337 + £0.2962 = £0.83 or 83p a day

24

So that's £0.83 x 365 = £302.91 a year before you use anything.

Next, they assume you will use 2900 kWhrs of electricity per year at £0.2735 per unit that's £793.15 for electricity.

Plus 12000 kWhrs of gas at £0.0689 per kWhrs or £826.80 for gas

In total its £826.90 + £793.15 + £302.91 = £1922 a year or £5.20 a day.

So, what who is this average household and what does it look like?

The average house is a 1930s, 3 bed, semidetached house with double glazing and loft insulation like this. Its floor area is 110m^2.

16 What is the best heat pump?

The most common question we get is "what's the best heat pump?

It's an interesting question, if I asked any manufacturer, they would always tell you it was their unit. Manufacturers tend to believe their own marketing.

The sad thing about heat pumps is they are all so incredibly similar, The SCOP (efficiencies), noise, size and colour are very similar. No one is miles ahead of anyone else. They all have the same features, none of them are stand out units despite the hype in the brochure. In our industry it is considered revolutionary to paint the unit a different colour and make a scene about it. Everyone tells you they offer amazing service and great prices with the best support.

My advice is always the same, you need to ask the installer what unit they like and use most. The installer is the person you are going to ring when you need your unit serviced, adjusted or when it makes a funny noise. If you push the installer into using a unit, they don't know don't be surprised that they can't help you. Your installer is an expert, he or she will work with suppliers they know and trust and don't let them down.

For example, I like Samsung units, I've worked on them for 13 years and know pretty much everything about them, I can remember all the faults, wiring, set up etc off the top of my head. So, for me a Samsung I the best unit in the world. Put me in front of a Daikin, LG Vaillant etc and I couldn't even turn it on, so for me they are not good units, and I would not recommend them.

And one last hint, the performance figures that are published on the MCS database and in the product, literature are what you can achieve if the unit is set up well and operated correctly. A bad set up will cost more to run and will be less comfortable. Make sure your installer knows how to get the best out of the unit and you will be warm and happy.

17 How can I tell if I have a 3-phase power supply?

In the UK almost every house has a 240Volt single phase power supply.

That means if you look at your electricity meter there are 2 cables coming into the meter and 2 cables going into the house, like this.

Note the grey cables comes out of the ground into the big black box on the right. This is the service fuse. You don't own this; the electricity company or district network operator owns it.

If you have a very large house or a commercial property it will look similar but there are 3 cables coming out of the ground and 3 going into the house, the meter will have 6 cables connected.

3 phase is not cheaper or better than single phase its just used for larger power supplies.

18 what is the advantage of a 3-phase power supply?

The problem with a normal single phase 240Volt power supply is its power limit is not very high. For example, if you have a 32 Amp power supply it will only be big enough to power a 16kW (output) unit.

If you had a 3-phase power supply giving a 32 Amp Supply would be able to power a 32 kW (output) heat pump.

So, 3 phase supplies can be used on bigger units.

In big houses this means you can use commercial units which are much cheaper than domestic units to install and buy.

SO instead of having 2 or 3 domestic heat pumps you can have one big commercial unit for a lot less money but only if you have a 3-phase power supply.

But don't be fooled, 2 phase electricity is just the same cost as single phase, it's not better, cleaner, or cheaper.

19 How do I know how drafty / leaky my house is?

Anyone who has lived in a house with wooden floors above an open cold void, think Victorian houses and those built up to the 1960s will tell you if you don't have a carpet the house will be freezing.

The reason is the cold air blowing around the floor void comes up into the house.

As you heat the air in your house it expands, the air then leaks out of the house and new fresh cold air comes in.

The speed at which the air enters your house is completely unknown. When we do a heat load calculation, we use guidelines to predict this.

Ventilation rate	AC/hr
2016-2020 regs	0.60
2006-2015 regs	0.70
Living rooms/Hallways	1.50
Dining rooms	1.50
Bedroom	1.00
Kitchen	2.00
Bathroom	2.00
Toilet	2.00

EXAMPLE

From the table above the air in the lounge of my 1930s house leaks so fast that all of it is replaced by cold air 1.5 times every hour. But if my house was new 2016-2020 for example it would be much more airtight at only 0.6 ai changes an hour.

Bizarrely if I move a bed into the same room and call it a bedroom it only leaks at a rate of 1 air change an hour. But in the absence of anything better this is what we use.

The proper way to determine how much air leaks out of and into the house is to measure it by doing an air tightness test.

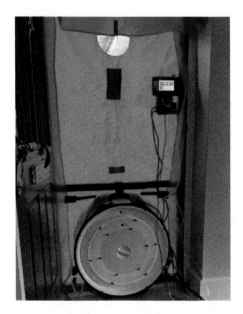

New buildings all have this done. The test involves opening the front door, putting a big fan in the hole, and pumping up the house to see how fast it leaks. It's a great idea to have this done, you can feel where the air is escaping and block up the worst leaks. Usually under the stairs, up the chimney and out the loft hatch.

Once you know the leakage rate you can much more accurately calculate the heat lost by warm air escaping out the house.

Less drafty = lower run costs and less CO_2.

20 Should I buy a battery, PV, a heat pump, or what combination of the above?

The real answer is probably yes, you should buy them all. But we must be realistic, most people can't or won't spend the money to have all these technologies installed in one go. Most people view the renewables road as a long and winding one.

It would be great if there was a simple answer to this, i.e. Do the heat pump first then battery then solar pv or some combination of the above. But it's nowhere near that simple.

Let me explain.Let's say you live in a 3 bed 1930s semi detached house. if you haven't modified it at all since buying it will be cold and drafty. Its heat loss will be something like 12kW and it will cost you £2500 a year to heat.

If you installed double glazing, loft insulation and cavity wall insulation this would drop to 9kW and £1900 a year.

So, it makes sense to do this first. If you put a heat pump in first its going to be big and expensive, once you insulate it will be too big for the job and a waste of money.

Putting solar PV on the roof is almost always a good idea, everyone uses electricity so making some of it yourself is a good idea. But how big a system is optimum. This obviously depends on how much electricity you use. Example if you have an electric car, you can charge it from the solar panels, if you don't you wont need as much electricity.

Batteries are a good idea if you have a variable tariff, mine is very expensive from 4-7 pm but cheaper all day and almost free in the middle of the night. So, charging the battery when electricity is cheap and using it when its expensive makes sense. But again, depends on how much energy you use.

In my Job we do this fiendishly difficult calculation for you, we take your energy usage and the insulation in your house and work out how much each system will cost, what its payback will be and what it will save you. You can even select them one at a time or mix and match to see how they interact with each other so you can plan your renewables journey.

You can try it free here www.genous.earth say Graham sent you.

21 Do I have to run my heat pump 24/7?

No. its your heat pump does with it what you please but bear this in mind.

I run my heat pump 24 / 7 7 days a week in Winter. My house is old and drafty and if its cold outside and I switch off the heating the house goes cold very quickly.

If your house is well insulated this effect will be greatly reduced.

Heat pumps are cheaper to run if you run them at lower temperatures, I say "you pay for the temperature".

If you run your heating all the time you can run the radiators warm to drip feed the heat into the building at the same rate it leaks out. Obviously the colder it gets the warmer the rads must be to maintain the same room temperature. This is weather compensation.

If you can't afford to run the heating all the time or are on a budget you might think lets just run the heating for 2 hours in the morning when you get up, switch it off all day and switch it back on to boost the house for when you get back in. Also makes no sense to heat it while you are asleep. There is nothing wrong with this argument but think about it.

If it's 5 degrees C outside I'm running my radiators at 40C to drip feed the heat into the building as my building never gets cold. If your heating has been off all day and its 5C outside your room temperature will be low, maybe 10 or 15 C, so you need to run the radiators a lot hotter to get the room up to 21C first and then maintain it there. You will have to thrash your heat pump to get it back up to temperature. And that cost more money.

So, running it for short periods is more expensive to do and less efficient. However, if you only run the heating for 4 hours a day it will always be cheaper than running it 24 / 7. It just won't be nearly as comfortable.

The cheapest way to run any heating system is to never turn it on, but that isn't comfortable at all.

I would recommend running the heat pump all the time but reduce the room temperatures from 21C to 18. It won't be super warm, but it will be ok, and you won't have condensation problems.

The secret is trying to maintain the house at the same temperature all the time. Hot-cold, hot-cold is never comfortable.

22 Why does it cost so much to heat old houses? And why does insulation help so much?

In my previous book, the purple one I discussed heat loss in detail. It's worth a look.

But in brief. Old houses are drafty see q 19, and badly insulated, unless they have been modified.

This is an example of a 120m^2 Victorian house.

Its total heat loss is 17.6kW, it loses 147 Watts for every m^2 of floor area.

Building Details		U-value	% of total heat lost
External Wall type	pre 1918 no cavity 9 inch brick	2.11	47%
Window type	pre 1990 single glazed wood	4.80	19%
Roof / Ceiling type	pre 1980 no insulation	1.50	13%
Floor type	pre 1918 wood floor with carpet	1.00	5%
Ventilation loss	Living rooms/Hallways	1.50	16%

if your house is built using more than one material its possible to enter this data for each room.

Note nearly half the loss is through the single skin walls.

Now if we move to a 1930s house and add double glazing and 200mm of lost insulation, look what happens.

Building Details		U-value	% of total heat lost
External Wall type	1970-1990 cavity wall 50mm insulation	1.00	41%
Window type	Double glazed wood/plastic	2.80	19%
Roof / Ceiling type	Pitched felt 200mm rockwool	0.20	5%
Floor type	pre 1918 wood floor with carpet	1.00	8%
Ventilation loss	Living rooms/Hallways	1.50	27%

if your house is built using more than one material its possible to enter this data for each room.

The heat loss from this building (same size as above) is now 10.5kW. the loss is 87W/m^2 of floor area. Its nearly twice as well insulated as the Victorian house so will cost ½ as much to heat,

Now let's look at a new build house.

Building Details		U-value	% of total heat lost
External Wall type	2020 - predicted building regs	0.18	29%
Window type	2020 - predicted building regs	1.40	25%
Roof / Ceiling type	2020 - predicted building regs	0.13	9%
Floor type	2020 - predicted building regs	0.13	7%
Ventilation loss	2016-2020 regs	0.60	31%

if your house is built using more than one material its possible to enter this data for each room.

This house has a heat load of only 4.2kW ¼ of that of the Victorian house.

It leaks heat at 36W/m^2.

Its run cost will be ¼ that of the old Victorian house and ½ that of a modified 1930s house. Insulation and draft proofing work, very well indeed.

23 Do I have to insulate my house first if I want a heat pump?

No, its your house you can do what you like. But look at q 22.

Adding double glazing, loft insulation and cavity wall insulation is relatively cheap. In some cases, it's free.

Double or secondary glazing is also effective.

There are some under floor insulation solutions which are very effective, some need the floors ripping up and insulation putting in the void but an overlay of insulation on the boards is also effective.

If you don't insulate you will need a big expensive heat pump (or boiler) to keep up with the heat leaking out the house. It will also be expensive.

Stopping the heat leaking out is more effective and means a smaller cheaper system. That's why they say insulate first.

Many firms including mine www.genous.Earth will calculate exactly what impact each measure will have, its best to work out the most effective and cheapest solutions first.

24 If I have a solar diverter should I switch off my heat pump in Summer?

Your heat pump consumes energy even when it's not running.

In Summer if you have a solar diverter heating the hot water cylinder your heat pump will not be required for heating (its warm outside) or hot water.

So how much does it cost to leave your heat pump plugged in but not running for 6 months?

Typically, the unit in the garden will draw between 10 to 20 Watts and the indoor unit / controls will draw 10 to 20 Watts.

That's a total of 40 Watts for the worst offenders.

40 Watts x 24 hours is just under 1kWhr of energy a day.

I pay £0.37 per kWhr of electricity.

So, it costs me £0.37 a day to leave it switched on which is £67 for half a year.

I turn my heat pump off at the mains in Summer and let the solar panels heat my water. Once a month I power up the heat pump for 10 minutes to let it spin the pumps and make sure nothing seizes inside. It's easy to save this money.

25 How do I measure how much my heat pump costs when it's not running?

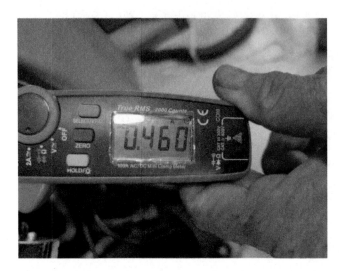

If you were to take the cover off your heat pump and use an Amp clamp you could see exactly how much energy it was using sitting, there doing nothing.

If you did this, you would get a reading not unlike this one above. 0.459 Amps.

At 240 Volts according to my schoolboy electrics I x V = Watts means the unit is drawing 230 Volts x 0.459 Amps = 106 Watts.

Yikes that's horrible. 106 x 24 hours means it uses 2.5kWhrs of electricity a day, at 33p a unit that's £0.83 a day, that's £303 a year.

Ok stop a second, if it was using this much current something would be hot, that 106 Watts must go somewhere. Last time I looked everything in the unit was cold or at least ambient temperature.

But before everyone panics there is a small issue with all the above, it's not true, your Amp clamp is assuming the Voltage across the unit is 230 Volts, but it's not, it's an induced Voltage, the unit is drawing 0.459 Amps but it's not at 230 Volts. When you are dealing with electronics and small currents you really need a Watt meter to measure what's going on (no pun intended).

If I put my Watt meter in circuit, you can see it using 14.1 Watts. A Watt meter measures both the current and the Voltage it does not assume anything.

Using an Amp clamp for this sort of measurement is not a good idea. Most heat pumps are now installed with a Watt or energy meter so you can see what's really going on. Insist your installer puts one in for you they are only £25.

26 How many kW hours of heat are in a cylinder of hot water, is it a battery?

Everyone is screaming about energy costs; wouldn't it help if we told the people what everything costs and let them make their own choices?

Heat maths isn't very hard, it's just a bit of addition, multiplication and most importantly getting the units right. We love a crazy unit in heatpumpery, it's a thin veil we hide behind to look clever and attractive.

Don't worry I'm not going to explain all here. I'm a big fan of making the maths much more accessible to our customers.

If you look at your gas or electricity bill or Meter, it reads in kWhrs. or Kilo Watt Hours.

Very few people know how big, or heavy a kWhr is, but they do know how much they pay for them. My house is 100% electric, so I pay 33p for every one of the little fellas I use.

A kilo Watt hour is the amount of energy you use if you turn on a 1000-Watt (a kilo Watt is 1000 Watts) heater, or light or fridge or anything else electrical for one hour. If you turn on a 3-kW kettle for 1 hour you use 3 kW hrs of energy, that's a quid in my house.

Here are a few useful rules of thumb for you to work out where your money is going.

How much does it cost to take a shower or bath in your house?

A 100 Litre bath or a10 minute shower uses 4 and 1/2 kWhrs of heat.

If you use electricity to heat that 100 Litres of water either in an electric shower or using an immersion heater it will consume 4 1/2 units, in my case 33p unit. That's £1.50

If you have a gas boiler it uses a bit more than 4 1/2 units of gas, your boiler is not 100% efficient, we will round it to 5 units. Gas is 7.5p a unit so its £0.35 for the same shower.

A heat pump is a bit better; we steal 2 free units of heat from the air in the garden for every 1 unit of electricity we use from the mains. So, to get our 4 1/2 units we squirt in 1.5 units at 33p a unit or 50p worth of electricity.

Your neighbour with the solar panel gets the electricity for nothing when its sunny, it makes no odds how he or she gets it into his hot water, it's free.

If you have a 300-litre hot water cylinder, it's not difficult to work out it will take 3 x 4 1/2 units or 13.5 kWhrs to heat it up once a day. That's £4.50 if you use normal electricity, £1 if you use gas and £1.50 for a heat pump.

Simple huh?

So, get out of the shower, don't fill the bath so high and don't leave the taps running, It's like the 70s again.

How much do electric appliances cost?

There are 9000 hours a year, if you plug anything electrical in and leave it on all year it uses 9 kWhrs for every Watt it draws.

Your phone charger is 10 Watts, it will use 90 kWhrs a year, that's £30 a year.

And that gas boiler you've got on the wall draws 90 Watts when its running, the damn thing would use 800 kWhrs of electricity a year if it was on 24/7 that's £267.

27 If I have a heat load calculation done on my house will it be accurate? Does it matter?

Let me explain. Heat loss calculations are done using rules laid down in the MCS standard. MCS police the government grants so everyone in the UK uses the MCS method.

We size every room in the house to operate at 21C, 24 hours a day,

The heat pump must be able to do this at least 99% of the time, we use a table to determine the design condition, example -1.8C at sea level in the Southeast of England. If the weather is lower than -1.8C the machine won't be able to maintain 21C in every room.

Put a simpler way we design the heat pump to be able to heat every room in the house to be 23.8C warmer than the temperature outside.

But we do this assuming there are no other heating appliances, so it's got to be in a dark, unoccupied house with no power on anywhere. We don't consider solar gain (it's not sunny at night) or any load in the house, cats, dogs, humans, kettles, TVs, lights etc.

In my house my background electrical load is 200 Watts (my total heat loss is 5kW), that electrical load alone meets 4% of my heat load. All of this goes into the house as heat.

Then there is us lot in the house, I'm 200 Watts, so is my Wife and the 2 cats must be 50 Watts each. That's another 500 Watts. We are just mobile heaters, so that's that's another 10% towards our heat loss. Taking this into consideration a heat pump which could provide 4300 of the 5000-Watt peaks would do the job.

But do you really keep all the rooms in your house at 21C all the time? if you are lucky enough to have a spare room maybe you could let this run colder on the coldest days of the year? If you ran the spare room colder this would reduce the heat load again.

Exhibit B: everyone does the same heat loss and then slightly over sizes the heat pump to cope. It's a rule of MCS.

This system below would fail.

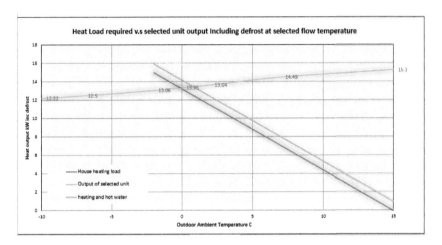

The red line is the heat load, the green line is the heat load plus hot water, and the blue is the real output of my chosen heat pump.

When it gets to 0 degrees C the heat pump capacity in blue falls below the red line. At this point it would not be able to meet the MCS design criteria.

So, this bigger unit would be better.

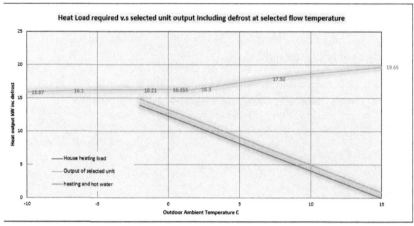

Heat Load required v.s selected unit output Including defrost at selected flow temperature

The rules of MCS state that the heat pump MUST be big enough for the job. MCS are the gatekeepers to the RHI (government grant) we have to use MCS approved calculations tif you want to recieve the grant. There is no flexibilty. You can see in the graph above that the heat we need, in red must lie below the heat pump outlet line in blue. The faint grey line shows how much heat we need for heating and hot water. The MCS calculation assumes you will heat EVERY room to the design temperature (typically 21C) 24 hours a day in heating season. All run costs and savings are based on this useage.

We MCS designers always go up a size to make sure we meet the demands and get our grants.

Exhibit C

If our heat loss was perfect and the heat pump output exactly matched what we needed, then in very cold snaps for the tiny number of hours the outdoor temperature fell below design, we would see the room temperatures were not able to make 21C even though the heat pump was flat out. Mrs Miggins (the homeowner) would call up and say, "last week my heat pump worked ok, now it's cold it doesn't, send a man". But this never happens. It's because we over size the unit, just in case.

So, we can see that we oversize a couple of times in the calculation, but what should we do?

Well, we carry on of course, while there is a grant to get, we will always work to insure whatever happens, we get the grant, but if there was no grant, we could try under sizing a bit. It's quite common is some other markets where MCS doesn't exist, but it's a brave game. If you get it wrong, you get a right roasting and its very expensive to fix.

28 What happens if my heat pump is undersized?

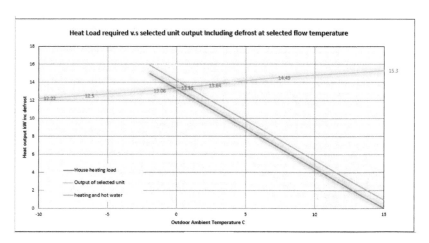

Let's image we have worked out your peak heat load to be14.5kW but you've bought a heat pump which only gives 13kW. See graph above.

Ther red line is heat needed, the blue line is unit capacity.

You can see that when the ambient temperature falls to 0 degrees C the unit is no longer big enough.

This is the definition of under sizing.

So, let's say we want the heat pump to maintain 21C in all rooms, this unit will heat to 21C in every room but only in ambient of 0 degrees and above.

If it gets to -2C outside the rooms will not get to 21C anymore. This unit can only hold the house 21 degrees hotter than the air outside. Normally we design so the unit can hold the house 22.8 degrees C above the ambient temperature in the South of England, and 25C in the North of Scotland.

If a heat pump is undersized, it just means eventually it won't be able to hold every room at the design temperature. The unit does not stop heating at 0C, its just not able to maintain room temperature. Its already flat out.

29 Why does everyone panic about pipe size? And should I do any tests before the heat pump company come to see us?

Heating Water pipes come in lots of sizes, from the smallest micro bore, the size of your kettle flex, trough to 15mm pipe the size of your middle finger and up to 22 mm pipe the size of a wine bottle neck with the cork in to 28mm pipe the size of a toothpaste tube.

All these pipes can carry hot water to and from your radiators.

The problem is that if the pipe is small, it can't carry the same amount of water as big pipes.

Its possible using big pumps to make the water move very quickly down the small pipes but if you do this you get lots of noise, like the noise you get when a tap runs.

So small pipes can deliver small amounts of water quietly and big pipes big amounts of water quietly.

In most houses you have 15mm middle finger size pipes feeding your rads. If you have this no pipework mods will be needed.

If you have little, tiny kettle flex size pipes its possible, but highly unlikely that you need to upgrade the pipes. BEFORE the plumber turns up do a test.

Run your boiler at 50 degrees C or mid temperature on the dial. Let it run for 10 minutes. Now go and feel every radiator in the house.

If the water is getting to all the rads they will all be about the same temperature. But look closer.

If the water is coming in too slowly only the left, right and top edges of the rad will be hot. IF the middle is cold the water speed is too low. Tell your installer what you found before they come to the house.

In most cases they can adjust the flow, so all the radiators get hot at the same time. IF this is impossible, they will have to get someone like me to run the maths and check that the pipes are an ok size.

The person surveying your house often doesn't have time to do this test, so why don't you do it and take them straight to the radiators that don't get hot or the coldest rooms in the house, they could sort these issues out while installing your new system.

30 Do I always have to replace my radiators? Can I try the old ones and replace them later if need be?

When your heating system was installed its possible that the heating engineer chose the radiators to operate at 70C flow temperature from your boiler and that you would run the heating for short periods and blast the heat into the room.

We are going to offer you a heat pump which can run like this but is much cheaper and greener to run low and slow.

Example: its much cheaper to run a heat pump for 8 hours with the radiators at 40 degrees C than it is to run it for 2 hours at 60 degrees C

So, you the homeowner have 3 options:

Keep running the system on the old rads for a couple of hours at a time but hot using a heat pump, it will work but it will cost 50% more than your boiler did.

Run your heat pump for much longer but at a lower temperature like 45C, it will be much more comfortable and will save you money.

Or go the whole hog and have your radiators upsized so you can run them at 35C, so you save even more money.

But before you decide, you can have your unit installed and replace the radiators one by one as you decorate, I did this, it took 6 years to replace all my radiators. As I replaced them, I slightly reduced the temperature and saved a lilt more energy.

Don't be fooled into doing everything all at once unless you want to. Its ok to replace the radiators after the heat pump and make gradual changes. In time you will have the ultimate system. Its your money, do what you like but make sure your installer tells you all the radiator sizes you will need and what sort of savings you will achieve. If they can't choose another installer.

31 What happens if I use my old cylinder and heat it with a diverter, will it work?

Most hot water cylinders have an immersion heater. Your solar diverter uses the free electricity from your solar panels to power the immersion instead of putting it back into the grid.

So, if you have an immersion heater in the cylinder its compatible with a solar diverter.

32 When I have a shower warm, water goes down the drain, can I recycle this heat?

It seems like a crazy idea to pay to heat a load of water, then shower in it, then throw it away down the plug hole even though it's still Lukewarm.

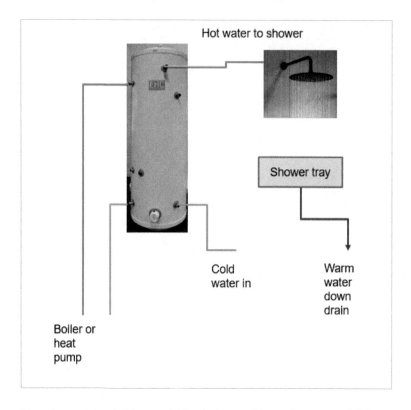

Hot water to shower

Shower tray

Cold water in

Warm water down drain

Boiler or heat pump

The clever thing to do would be to try and recycle some of this heat and use it to pre warm the cold water filling up the hot water cylinder.

This is what a shower save does.

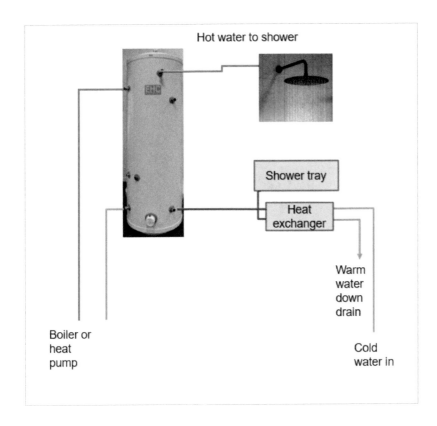

Hot water to shower

Shower tray

Heat exchanger

Warm water down drain

Boiler or heat pump

Cold water in

The warm shower water runs down a drainpipe with another pipe inside which brings in the cold water.

The end s=result is that the water from the mains comes in at 10C, its warmed by the shower water on its way to the drain. The water enters the tank at 20C, and it costs nothing to run.

In recent trails on my sons house he reclaims 33% of his hot water this way. A shower save is a simple technology which works and has no moving parts and needs no maintenance. It makes perfect sense.

https://www.showersave.com/product

33 Can I trust the heat meter readings in my heat pump controller?

In the UK we do not have to measure or report the efficiency of any heating device accurately. There is no boiler anywhere which measures the heat produced or the gas consumed. And they don't measure how much electricity the boiler uses to provide your heating. In fact, you just assume your efficiency based on the fictional figures you are given when you buy the boiler. 90% efficiency is apparently, that is a triumph of marketing.

We in heat pump land are a bit better than that, but we are not perfect, we use some devices which help the figures. Its common now in heat pumps to measure energy in and heat out and give you a COP figure on screen. But most heat pumps only measure the power drawn by the compressor, we conveniently forget about the controls, pcb, fans, pumps etc. so the figure is reported slightly higher than is real.

You could put special dedicated heat meters on the pipework and measure the actual energy the whole system uses and get a really accurate figure for COP, but it's not a requirement and is strictly for geeks.

The point is to be careful when you see any COP claim which looks high, if it looks high it probably is not completely true. The figures for your machine on the MCS product database and in the literature is a true representation of what you are really going to achieve.

As an example, these are realistic SCOP figures for a whole heating season at each of the design or run temperatures. IF you are achieving these levels, you are doing very well indeed.

design temp	scop @design temp
40	5.24
50	4.38
60	3.8

Word of caution, DON'T look at your cop every day, it will rise and fall with the weather. These figures are averages across a 6-month heating cycle.

34 How and why does my heating cost alter over the year? Or why is my run cost so high in Winter?

Ok first things first your heating bill varies month by month. Its expensive to heat in Winter, cheaper in Autumn and Spring and free (the heating is off) in Summer. But you pay a flat bill by direct debit every month. In Summer you overpay and end up in credit, in Winter you underpay and burn the credit off.

In Q18 we talked about the average house. If we look at this house after the gas boiler has been removed and the new heat pump is installed this table above is a very typical run cost profile for the house if it was heated 24/7 to 21 degrees C in every room.

Below is a table of run cost per month, or what you use each month in this house.

The total £1263 bill would be covered by a direct debit of (816.69 + 447.14) / 12 = £106 per month or £3.50 a day.

Run cost per month of heat pump		heating cost / month		Hot water cost / month	
Month	% energy used/ month				
January	20%	£	163.34	£	37.26
February	17%	£	138.84	£	37.26
March	12%	£	98.00	£	37.26
April	7%	£	57.17	£	37.26
May	4%	£	32.67	£	37.26
June	2%	£	16.33	£	37.26
July	0%	£	-	£	37.26
August	0%	£	-	£	37.26
September	4%	£	32.67	£	37.26
October	6%	£	49.00	£	37.26
November	12%	£	98.00	£	37.26
December	16%	£	130.67	£	37.26
total	100.00%	£	816.69	£	447.14

Note I've split the heating and the hot water costs. But as an example, In January you use £163+ £37 = £200 or £6.50 a day.

In July you use £37 or just over £1 a day.

The golden rule is don't take your peak day or months usage and multiply up for the year, that makes no sense. You can use the percentage figures above to estimate your years bill, it works well. The data comes for 13 years of recording my usage at home.

Hot water usage and cost is flat it costs the same as you use the same amount of hot water all the time. The block in yellow represents the part of the hot water you could heat using solar diverters on your hot water cylinder. If you do this these costs fall to £0.

35 What is freeze up prevention and how does it work?

Your heat pump lives outside, its horrible out there, if its freezing cold the unit needs to protect itself from the elements and you. The pipework is full of water which if it gets cold enough will freeze. If it freezes inside the unit, it can cause quite a lot of damage which means no heating and an insurance claim.

Over the last 13 years in heat pumps, I've known 2 units to freeze up, out of over 10000 we supplied. Both were being messed around with by the homeowner, heat pumps just like oil boilers, don't freeze up.

All heat pumps have several cold weather protection functions these include:

The heat pump is terrified that the water might drop below 10C, if the unit detects the heat exchanger is less than 10C it does two things:

Firstly, the water pump is switched on for a couple of minutes to bring water in from the system indoors to maintain the temperature in the unit. You might witness this on cold nights, if you can hear your water pump it might run for a minute or two every couple of hours just making sure nothing freezes up. This function costs a few pence a day. Ignore it. You cannot turn this off.

Secondly In really cold weather, if its less than -2C outside the unit will run the water pump continuously, you probably won't notice, if it's that cold the heating will be running anyhow.

Thirdly, if it's cold, the water pump has been running and the water in the system is still cold below 10C the heat pump will start and run for a few minutes and raise the water temperature back up to 20C. Even if you have turned the unit off at the thermostat. You must think if the water in the rads is below 20C the house must be very cold. This function you often only see in houses which are not occupied, and the heating has been left switched off.

Some installers use Glycol (anti-freeze) and freeze up valves on the system as even further protection. These are belt and braces solutions just in case there is freezing weather and a power cut at the same time.

58

36 WRAS heat pumps and hot water only solutions.

In many circumstances we get asked to build heat pump solutions for sports clubs, restaurants, and commercial premises where they want a hot water only heat pump.

The biggest problem with these systems is cost followed by efficiency.

The problem is we need a heat pump outside connected to a heat pump cylinder to hold the water. The limiting factor is always the Sze of the coil in the cylinder. The manufacturers can only squeeze so much coil inside the cylinder body. Many installers use a plate heat exchanger and pump outside the cylinder which separates the water circulating through the heat pump from the water in the cylinder. But this is expensive and you loose heat across the plate heat exchanger.

The ultimate system would have the water from the cylinder being directly heated by the heat pump. Let me cover that again, the water you bathe in would go through the heat pump itself and be warmed up directly.

To do this is easy, anyone can tube this up, but understandably the heat pump, the pipes and all the plumbing components need to be clean. Hot water systems are covered by a regulation called WRAS, the water regs. Every component the water you bath in touches must be certified and tested.

A company in Fareham called d RJC mechanical modify a Samsung heat pump to make it WRAS compliant, they do a range of WRAS approved heat pumps which heat hot water only, I've not seen them anywhere else.

The installation is child splay. RJC ME sell you a heat pump, water pump, flow switch, controls, stats and a cylinder and you tube it up. It's all preset up, so you turn it on and leave. It's a beautiful solution. It looks like this.

RJC ME WRAS / Kiwa heat pump hot water installation

The DHW water runs through the heat pump direct into the cylinder. Simple, efficient and fast to install.

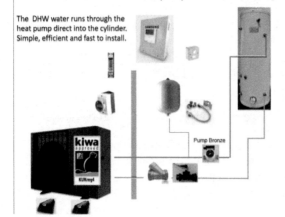

Pump Bronze

RJC 12 or 14kW Samsung Kiwa approved heat pump
Mim-E03CN control box with WRAS approved flow switch
8m Bronze WRAS approved water pump
Strainer WRAS approved
Flexi connections WRAS approved x 2

Also required:
2 x pump valves 28mm
Cylinder
Feet x 2
32 Amp isolator
Electric meter x 1
Fused spur 13 Amp x 1
Robokit 18 l white

www.rjcme.com

37 Can I heat my house and my swimming pool with the same heat pump?

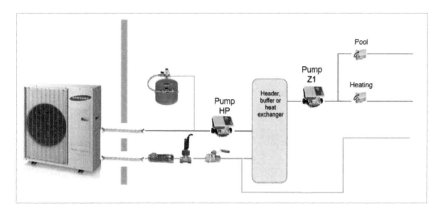

Heating a pool and a house is simple, the pool and the house each have a zone valve and controls and when heating is required the hot water goes where it's needed.

Its no different from a system which as 2 or more zones in a house, for example an upstairs and downstairs heating zone.

The problem is the pool.

Pools tend to be run at a water temperature of 30C. this is much lower temperature than the radiators in the heating circuit. The pool also has a near infinite capacity to soak up heat.

If in the example above both the pool and the house were heated together the pool would suck up all the heat and the radiators would not get to temperature.

If your heating engineer is very skilled at balancing, they can drip feed the pool and send lots of heat to the house suing balancing valves. But it's hard to do.

My advice is, if the pool is only used in summer when the heating is off the system above is ideal. If you have an indoor pool which is used all year round ALWAYS put a separate heating system in for the pool and another for the house, don't connect them together.

38 Can I run my heat pump to work with my variable / flexible electricity tariff?

Electricity tariffs come and go so choosing the right one is tricky.

Currently in December 2023 there is one called Octopus Cosy.

The way it works is there is a normal day rate, a cheap rate, and an expensive rate. The average cost over 24 hrs is the day rate.

time	hrs	p/kWhr		
0-4	4	£ 0.28	£	1.10
4 to 7	3	£ 0.17	£	0.50
7 to 13	6	£ 0.28	£	1.65
13-16	3	£ 0.17	£	0.50
16-19	3	£ 0.44	£	1.32
19-24	5	£ 0.28	£	1.38
total	24		£	6.44

£ 0.27

The idea is you heat the house when its cheap, i.e. 4-7 am and 1- 4 pm, don't run the heating between 4 and 7 pm and save loads of money.

Its quite easy to do with a simple time clock and thermostat, set the heating to turn up after lunch to 22C get the house warm, turn it back down to 19C from 4pm till 7pm, then back up to 21C from 7pm till 1 pm the next day.

Remembering also to run the dishwasher, the hot water cycle, the washing machine etc between 4 and 7 am and 1 and 4 pm only.

It's easy to get used too.

If you buy a smart controller from Homely, it will log into your tariff and automate the heat pump operation to do just this.

If you have this sort of tariff don't just leave the heating on and use it 24/ 7 at the same temperature, you won't make any savings.

39 Should I have a smart meter if I want renewables at home?

Quite simply put, yes!

I would go as far as to say if you don't want a smart meter, I would consider whether renewables are really for you, the two work in harmony together.

If you don't have a smart meter, you can't access any of the variable tariffs, you can't get any money for any excess solar you produce and you can't see what you are using.

I don't understand why anyone doesn't want a smart meter. But it's your choice sees q38, without a meter you can't have this tariff.

40 Will the grid cope if we all go for heat pumps?

83% of the houses in the UK are heated by Gas. The plan is to get these people to move over to electricity and heat pumps.

IF all this heat is switched from Gas to electricity will the grid cope. Well, if everyone switched over tomorrow, probably not.

Its pretty clear the electricity providers are going to need to put more power generation in place, hence wind farms and solar farms and possibly more cables.

But there are two reasons I'm relaxed about this:

The first is I don't make or distribute power, there are far cleverer people than me at national grid who I'm sure are working on a solution and as such its none of my business.

And secondly, I think the grid will be restructured over the next few years. Right now, the model is to make electricity at big central power stations and distribute this over a grid or web to all the houses. But as we all install solar Pv batteries and electric cars (these are just batteries on wheels) we could feed power back into the web and out across the country. Its like decentralised power generation. You will be able to store energy in your car and then use it to drive the lights and heat pump in high price periods, you will also be able to sell the surplus into the grid at a premium.

There is already work going on to pool all the power generation is some areas and sell it into the grid on an organised scale, you will see models like this coming soon. The idea being your road or cul-de-sac will group together and trade with each other and as a group with the web. Its exciting times for this technology.

So, I'm not worried about this at all, where there is a need, a solution will come forward.

41 Why are there so many types of heat pump?

I covered this in brief in book 2 but here's more info.

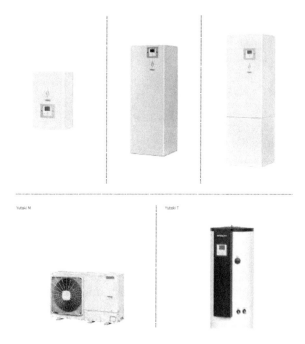

Yutaki M   Yutaki T

online.

Heat pumps are all the same, they are simple machines which have 4 essential components. They are:

The compressor, it's the refrigerant pump which does all the work. It's always inside the unit in the Garden.

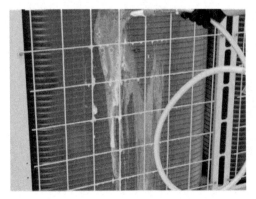

The next part is the outdoor unit coil we use to harvest the free heat from the garden, we fridge engineers call it an evaporator, just to make life complex in air conditioning this same coil is called a condenser. It's the blue coil on the back of the outdoor unit.

Next, we have a valve to control the refrigerant movement, it's called an electronic expansion valve, it's basically an electronic version of the valve on your radiators.

And finally, we need a heat exchanger which allows the hot refrigerant, to warm the water without the two mixing. These are called plates, plate heat exchangers or HEX. They have refrigerant one side and water the other so technically we should call them refrigerant to water heat exchangers, they look like this.

Where we put this component determines what type of heat pump you have.

There are 2 very distinct types of heat pumps:

A monobloc unit is defined as a unit which has all four of these refrigerant components housed in one box delivered to site as a complete system. Monobloc units are designed for heating engineers, who connect water pipework up to the unit outside, its simple just like a boiler, but it lives in the garden. The advantage with Monoblocs is they are simple, and any plumber can connect them up using their skills and tools, but pumping water up and down the garden is expensive, the pipes are large, so these systems like to be installed close to the house.

Water to the outdoor unit using insulated water pipes

Good for heating engineers and when the unit can be close to the house

A split unit is defined as a unit which does not have all four of the refrigerant components inside, the compressor, expansion valve and evaporator are in the box which lives outside, the refrigerant to water heat exchanger comes in another box which goes inside the house, So the unit comes in two pieces which is why we call it a split. The two pieces are connected using refrigerant pipework, not water pipework.

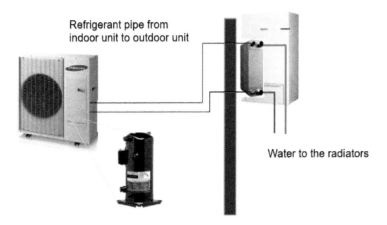

Refrigerant pipe from indoor unit to outdoor unit

Water to the radiators

Splits are designed for air-conditioning engineers. They are super popular in Southern Europe where the air conditioning engineers have no work in Winter, so they get involved in heating.

A split unit needs both a heating engineer and a refrigeration or FGAS engineer to install them. The FGAs engineer installs the fridge pipework between the two boxes, the heating engineers connect water pipework up to the indoor unit, which looks exactly like a boiler. We give it a stupid name; we call it a hydro box.

Splits have the advantage that it's very easy to run refrigerant pipes long distances for a relatively low cost. Decent split units can go 75m down the garden with very little loss of heat.

Neither mono or splits are more efficient, and neither is better.

That's the major classes explained, In the water side of the system, we like:

an expansion vessel to take up the slack as the water cools and heats.

A water pump to move the water round the house.

And a flow switch which measures if the water is moving and if so, how fast.

A filter to keep all the crap out of the heat exchanger, this would block it up,

Every heat pump on the planet needs all these bits too. The only difference between the different heat pumps is where the manufacturers decide is best to place them.

The simplest units have **none** of these components inside, the plumber must install them all somewhere in the house. Samsung and Mitsubishi do this. I call it self-assembly.

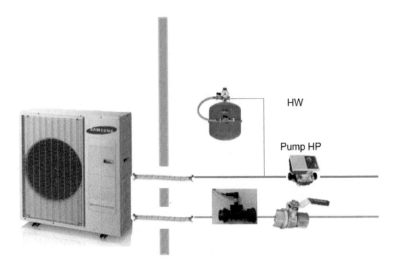

HW

Pump HP

Because this can be a pain to do on site manufacturers often screw all these bits on the front of the hot water cylinder to make the plumbers work easy, it's called pre plumbing, or laziness. See below.

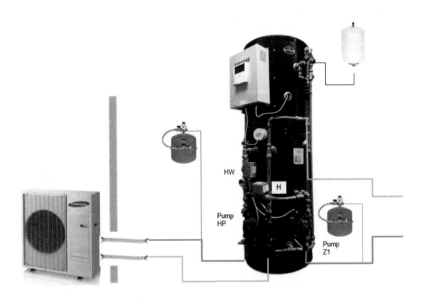

HW

Pump
HP

Pump
Z1

H

Some monobloc units have these parts included inside the box in the garden, it makes them easier to install but physically bigger. Panasonic, Midea etc.

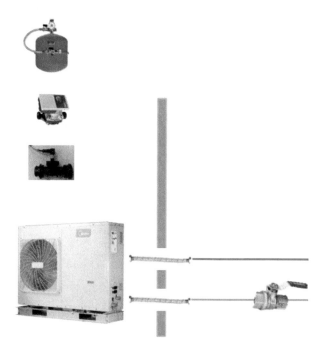

Hydro Splits

To make matters more complex there is a new breed of monobloc heat pump, you connect the water to the unit in the garden just like before, but the manufacturer puts all the plumbing components in a separate boiler shaped box inside the house. I call this a wet split. Brilliantly the indoor unit is also called a hydro box.

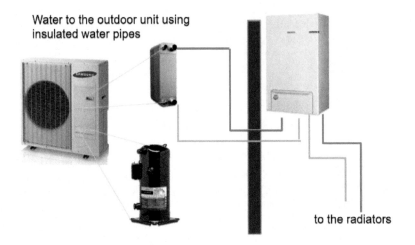

Water to the outdoor unit using insulated water pipes

to the radiators

The only major difference between the units is geography, i.e. where are all the bits housed. The way they work, efficiency etc is all the same.

It's a bit like cars, you can have the engine in the front, the middle, or the back, its still a car.

42 I keep seeing incredible COP figures online, should I trust them and what the theoretical maximum?

A heat pump is just a machine which can move heat and therefore lift the temperature from one place to another using a refrigerant and a pump. Your fridge does it, it sucks heat out of your frozen pizza and moves it out the back and heats your kitchen. Moving or pumping heat is not creating any energy, it's just moving it.

There is a formula for working out what the absolute theoretical efficiency you can achieve if the heat pump is perfect and has no friction etc. It's called the Carnot efficiency, Carnot discovered this rule, he did not write it, it's a law of physics and is totally unbreakable. The formula is simple:

The maximum achievable efficiency is the temperature of the hottest part of the system (+273 because they loved Kelvin as a temperature scale back in the day) divided by the difference in temperature between the hottest bit and the coldest bit.

example:

My heat pump is working at 10C outside, which is 283K, inside its heating the water to 40C or 313K. The efficiency in theory could be 313/ (313-283) = 10.4

Tcold C		Tcold K	Thot C		Thot K	Delta T	Efficency
10		283	40		313	30	10,43

Great news for marketeers, but it's not completely true. The problem is if its 10C outside the heat pump must work at a slightly lower temperature to absorb the heat, remember hot goes to cold. So, we run our heat pump coil at 2C when its 10C outside. The same is true for the inside part heating the water. To make water at 40C we must run the heat pump at a higher temperature something like 43C. So now the formula changes to:

efficiency in theory could be 316/ (313-275) = 7.7

Tcold air C	T cold refrigerant	Tcold K	Thot C	Thot refrigerant	Thot K	Delta T	Efficency
10	2	275	40	43	316	41	7.71

That's more like it. If the heat pump was perfect, we could achieve a cop of 7.71 in these conditions.

But Carnot didn't have to worry about powering water pumps, printed circuit boards, crankcase heaters or fan motors and he assumed compressor efficiency was 100%. There is no way you can get anything like this good efficiency in these conditions. It would be more reasonable to achieve a COP of 5 from any heat pump running in the conditions listed above.

Most of the incredible COP claims are for very short run times on lovely warm days with tepid radiator temperatures, like this, note it's been running for 1 hour with an instant COP of 7.21 but over the hour its

☰ 3.2 Performance Summary			⟨ ⟩
	Average		Instantaneous
Renewable heat generated	0.012 MWh		9.813 kWh
Electric consumed	0.001 MWh		1.360 kWh
SCoP / CoP	6.45		7.21
Number of starts	4		
Number of defrosts	0		
Heating runtime	0 days	1 hrs	
Hot water runtime	0 days	0 hrs	
Backup boiler runtime	0 days	0 hrs	
Time since last reset:	0 days	3 hrs	

6.45.

See Q 33 for more realistic figures. The same unit above looked like this after a year running.

☰ 3.2 Performance Summary		⟨ ⟩
	Average	Instantaneous
Renewable heat generated	8.180 MWh	5.763 kWh
Electric consumed	3.054 MWh	1.305 kWh
SCoP / CoP	2.67	4.41

43 How should I look after my heat pump? ACF50

Heat pumps and aircon units are subject to some terrible conditions, I think it's time to give them some love.

Your heat pump sits outside the house in all weathers, sun, rain, and snow. If you don't look after them eventually, they fade and start to look tired and unloved, just like you would if you laid out in the weather all day without a bit of moisturiser.

If you live by the sea like I do, in Southampton it's even worse.

Eventually the sea air and spray will rust the metalwork of the unit, despite the claims of the manufacturers, who all treat their coils with special coatings, the tin work is going to rust. Its life.

Please ignore all the claims like "our unit doesn't rust, it's got the newfangled bullshit coating on it", it hasn't, they only coat the coils, we all know it, the casing is going to rust.

In Saline conditions you need to have your unit coated with Bronzglow or Blygold, they are like varnishes which protect the paintwork. Some manufacturers do this for you as an option.

If you forget, or you are in a rush to install, or an idiot drills holes in the unit to put the cables in, it ruins the paint coatings. So, the units rust.

I advise everyone maintaining heat pumps spray every unit with ACF50 once a year no matter where its installed,

ACF50 is like pink olive oil, you spray it on and wipe it over the unit with a rag. It comes up shiny. You can use it on metal or plastic, and it looks amazing.

Once you are into ACF50 you start spraying it on your tools and everything else. I use it on all my motorbikes, and they gleam, avoid using it on the brakes though, trust me.

Welcome to a richer life with ACF50 in it, enjoy it and welcome to a rust-free shinier life. P.S Amazon sell it.

44 What's the best compressor in a heat pump?

Every heat pump has a compressor, It's the big black thing at the bottom of the unit which buzzes away when the units running. Most of them are wrapped up in a jacket to make them quiet. The one in the picture is an extreme example, you would find that in a 1 Mega Watt heat pump. The one in your unit looks more like this, but not gold. The compressor is just a pump, it takes low pressure refrigerant gas and compresses it, typically by about 4 times into a high pressure, hot gas. It's this hot gas we are going to use to heat the water in our heat pump.

The motor and the compressor parts are all mounted in a steel shell or crankcase, which is designed to be able to hold the maximum pressure in the unit, typically up to 40 bar. It's between 1 and 2mm thick.

Compressors in domestic heat pumps fall into two types, both of which are patented so they are all very similar when you look inside. The compressors we use in this industry are either swing / rotary type, favoured in small units and at the cheaper end of the spectrum and scrolls in big units or at the more expensive end. Scrolls are expensive to make so they are often avoided to keep costs down.

Both look identical from outside the only way to tell is cut the thing open with an angle grinder.

On the left is a scroll compressor. You need to google a video of how it works, its too hard to draw.

And on the right, is a rotary compressor. These compressors are very

simple see below.

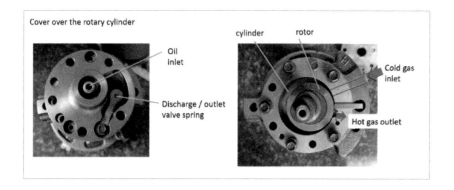

Cover over the rotary cylinder

Oil inlet

Discharge / outlet valve spring

cylinder   rotor

Cold gas inlet

Hot gas outlet

And simple to explain how they work. See the 5 images below as I turn the compressor through 1 turn.

At the beginning the whole cylinder is full of cold gas

As the rotor turns anti clockwise its pushing the gas forward.

At the middle of the turn it both bringing in cold gas at the top and compressing hot gas, bottom.

Here the hot gas is highly compressed and will start to exit the compressor.

At the end of the rotation the gas has all been pushed out and we are well into the next cycle.

The simplicity is a good idea, my compressor at home has completed just under 3000 hours of operation or 500 million rotations this year your compressor will turn 6 billion times in its life.

45 Modulation and inverters? What does that mean?

My house has a 6kW load when its 21 degrees inside and -2 degrees C outside. Today its 15 degrees C outside so the load I need to keep my house at 21C is small, something like 1kW. If I had a 6kW fixed speed heat pump it would be on and off, cycling because it's too big for the job today. Heat pumps don't like working like this. We like to keep the number of starts down to reduce wear on the compressors.

In boilers, modulating boilers have been around for years. Modulation or capacity control is quite hard to do in a boiler, if you turn the flame down too far it goes out. It's not uncommon for boilers to only be able to give between 50 and 100% of maximum rated capacity unless they are very clever with multiple burners etc. If you stand outside you can hear your neighbour's boiler going on and off every few minutes. Boilers seem to be ok cycling on and off again and again.

To reduce the problem of cycling in fixed speed heat pumps they used to put a buffer vessel in the circuit. A buffer is a big bucket of water, think of it as a heat battery. The fixed speed unit would thrash away and heat the buffer till it was warm. Then it would stop. The battery / buffer would provide the heat for the house for 15 minutes or so and then the unit would recharge it. But there is a much cleverer solution.

Back in ancient times, (pre-1985) all air-conditioners were also fixed speed. If you bought a 10kW unit, it gave 0 kW when it was off and 10kW when it was on. If the unit was big sometimes, they used 2 compressors so you could have no power, half power or full power. It was horrible. In the late 80s the Japanese manufacturers introduced a thing called an inverter drive to the air con world. It enabled the speed of the compressor in the system to be controlled up and down to suit the load. The unit could be off or rev up to 100% in tiny steps. It was a revelation, it made the units much better, the power supplies much smaller, the efficiency higher, the temperature control was better, and the compressors were more reliable.

It took about 10 years before Inverter driven aircon units became the norm, mostly because it took that long for them to be priced at the same level as fixed speed machines. Now inverter technology is widespread, every electric car, solar PV system, most vacuum cleaners and washing machines have this sort of motor drive in them.

46 Recirculation pumps for hot water.

Heat pumps cannot heat water instantly, they have inbuilt time delays and not enough capacity to heat water instantaneously, so we always use domestic hot water cylinders with this technology.

Anyone who lives in a big house knows that it can take quite a while for the hot water to make it to the taps from the hot water cylinder. There is a regulation that it should take less than 30 seconds to come out hot.

The accepted solution for this problem is to put a hot water ring main all around the house and a pump on it. The pump takes water from the cylinder and pushes it round the house so it's much closer to the taps. When you turn on the hot water tap out comes lovely warm water.

You can tell if you have this system because next to your cylinder there will be a re-circulation pump like this. They are usually orange. You will also probably be paying a fortune to heat your house and hot water.

Re-circulation pumps are a really good solution, but in almost every case its badly applied. let me explain.

The hot water loop is usually copper pipe, it is very rarely insulated (it should be) this acts as a radiator, slowly heating the house. The hot water comes back to the cylinder a bit colder. In time the cylinder temperature falls and the boiler or in my case the heat pump must re heat it.

If there is no re circulation pump, we might have to do 1 or 2 hot water cycles a day, but with a re circulation pump fitted it could be we have to do 10 or more cycles. In winter this is not so bad as the heating would be on anyway, but in spring, summer, and winter it's just burning money.

We engineer usually set them up, so the pump is on 24 hours a day, it's not our money and we don't want you ringing us up saying that it took ages for the hot water to come out of the shower. Run it 24/7 and you, the end user is happy until you see the bill.

But the sensible thing to do would be get the pump to run for the smallest possible period, literally a few minutes a day. Ideally the pump should start a few minutes before you jump in the shower and stop as soon as you are finished, it should not be running all the time you are at work and all the time you are asleep.

And then the triple whammy, with a heat pump we use immersion heaters to help us if the heat pump is taking too long to heat the cylinder. In normal applications the immersion is rarely used except for the legionella cycle, but with a re circulation pump the hot water demand is massive and the unit is constantly struggling to keep up. You are heating the tank with an immersion, which in turn is heating the re circulation loop, which is heating the house. all by direct electricity. So, your average hot water bill has now risen from £100 a year to 3,4 or 5 hundred pounds a year.

The solution:

The big pump manufacturers make intelligent recirculation pumps, they learn your hot water usage and only operate a few minutes at a time to support that usage. These are an amazing idea. They retail for less than £200, fit in place of the standard pumps and will save their own cost in a matter of months.

47 Are heat pumps noisy, an update.

When I wrote my first book on heat pumps, I compared the noise from a heat pump as similar in level to a microwave oven with a desk fan. But over the last 2 years heat pumps have had a major change.

Firstly, they have got shorter in height but fatter and wider. The extra depth is needed to hold lots of noise absorbing foam.

The bigger casing also allows manufacturers to have one big fan instead of two small fans.

The new fans have serrated edges, bumps, and lumps on them all to reduce the noise. The latest heat pumps are now quieter than a gas boiler.

Older unit   **new unit**

Noise is no longer an issue with these units. In most cases until they are flat out its difficult to tell they are running.

48 How does a heat pump work?

In our industry we have a problem with explaining what we do simply, so I am going to have a go. Hold on it might be riveting.

I am a lucky guy; I have a freezer at home. I chose a SMEG because I think the name is funny, I liked Red Dwarf. I was gutted when I found out it was just an LG with a fancy door on it but don't tell anyone else.

My freezer is amazing, I can take some hot cross buns, put them inside, close the door and a few hours later they are frozen solid. Contrary to popular belief there is nothing magic going on here.

Under all that ice in the freezer there are some silver tubes, inside the tubes is a refrigerant, its nothing fancy, my freezer uses a refrigerant called propane, heat pump geeks call it R290, it's the stuff you use to fuel your barbeque. you can buy it in B and Q.

All Refrigerants have one amazing quality, they can absorb enormous amounts of heat and can be moved around efficiently. In my freezer the propane is very cold, it literally sucks the heat out of anything near it, in my case those hot cross buns. Hot goes to cold, it's the law. (sorry I had to put one thermodynamics joke in).

The refrigerant is moved around the freezer using a pump, it's the buzzy thing that looks like a black football on the back. It's quite literally an electrically driven pump, we fridge engineers think we are clever, so we call it a compressor, it's a pump.

The pump sucks in the cold refrigerant (now full of hot cross bun heat) and compresses it, compressing it is a bit like wringing out a sponge. The heat is squeezed out of the refrigerant, and it's pumped through the black coil on the back of my freezer where the heat is dumped into my kitchen. Once the refrigerant is cooled off it returns through a valve very like the one you see on a radiator, it enters the freezer into the cold pipes again. The refrigerant is never used up, it just goes round and round again and again.

So, to recap, I suck heat out of my hot cross buns and dump the heat into my kitchen. I'm quite literally heating my kitchen with a combination of electrical power and heat from my food. If I was a clever dick I wouldn't call it a freezer, I would call it a food to kitchen heat pump.

so what? What's this got to do with heat pumps?

Simple, DO NOT TRY THIS AT HOME, if I took my freezer outside and ripped the doors off it would now cool down the air in the garden, the heat from the air would get sucked into the refrigerant, (remember hot goes to cold) the refrigerant would go through the pump, get squeezed and the heat would be discharged out of the back of the freezer. If I was to drizzle water over the black coil at the back of the freezer and collect it at the bottom it would be lovely and warm, I could run inside with the bucket and pour it through my radiators. And then I could call it an air to water heat pump. That is quite literally all there is too it.

An air source heat pumps is a massive freezer which cools the garden and heats water, you don't even need a bucket, we do that bit for you too. There is nothing new in this technology, I have had a freezer since I was a kid.

My freezer has been running for 11 years at a constant -19 degrees C. It's never been maintained, it's never broken down, it just goes on and on and on.

Heat pumps are also not new technology, they are simple machines using freezer technology that everyone knows, works, you have one at home already.

49 Why your heat pump weather comp is set to 37 degrees, The Lizzie curve.

I put my first heat pump in at home in 2009, it was a Daikin split Altherma. There was no MCS and no guidance at all from any external sources, we did whatever we liked. The heat pump went in and even though we didn't need to back then, we did a heat loss on every room and checked the radiator sizes. Most of the rads were resized as we refurbished the house, and the heat pump was set to go.

If you are intelligent and amazing at maths, you can work out exactly how to set the weather comp curve for your house, if not you follow the guidelines given in the manual. Because there were no guidelines back in 2009, I guessed the curve and set the unit up.

My house needs to be heated as soon as it gets to 15 degrees C outside in the garden, we call this the ambient temperature. So, I set my radiators to be at 25 degrees C when it was 15C outside. I designed my system to be flat out when it was -2 degrees C outside, so I set my radiators to run at 50C when it was that cold. This is called weather compensation.

The problem was although the curve made sense to mathematicians it didn't make sense to my wife Lizzie. Firstly, she moved into a drafty old house with a stupid new boiler which runs the radiators stone cold. She hated it. I was asked again and again why although the house was warm why were the radiators so cold?

I got so fed up with questions I altered the weather compensation, so the radiators never ran less than 37C or blood temperature. If you touch a radiator when its less than 37C it feels dead and cold, at 37C magic happens, it feels like the heating is on.

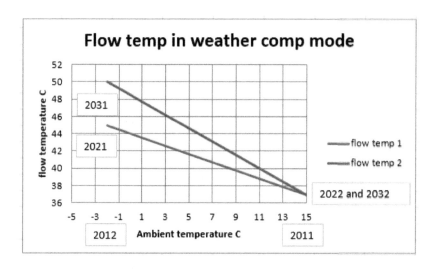

From that day on every manual, I ever wrote told the engineers to set the temperature to 37C when it was 15C outside and 50C when it was -2C outside. Not the perfect curve, not the cheapest curve, but the happiest, or the Lizzie curve. It seems to have caught on.

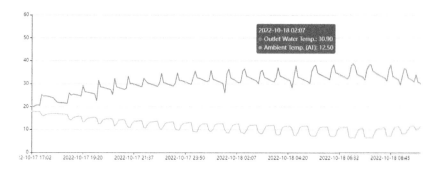

Note how the unit is cycling a bit in this graph, it's because I have set the radiators just a bit too warm, I need to tweak it down, also note how as the temperature falls outside the radiators get warmer. this is weather comp in action. I'm slowly tweaking the weather compensation settings down to get it better. It's taken weeks so far. This is not something anyone, but a lunatic would try at home. Yes, it's more perfect than the Lizzie curve, but its lots of work. This is exactly what Homely and the other heat pump optimisers do for you, they the unit to get the very best out of it.

50 How long do heat pumps last?

On 17th November 2011 the world's first prototype Samsung monobloc heat pump was installed, it was at my house. I still have the unit in my

museum of heatpumpery, it's one of my most prized possessions.

In March 2012 the unit was officially launched at the Mostra Convegna exhibition in Milan.

They even had a pre plumbed cylinder to show. We didn't adopt it here in the UK. It took us another 3 years to re-invent the idea here.

The first units went out the door in June 2012. This one was in

Aberdeenshire, I commissioned it. It's still running.

This is the earliest photo I have of an installation commissioned by the installer themselves; it was in July 2013. 13 years ago. It's still running.

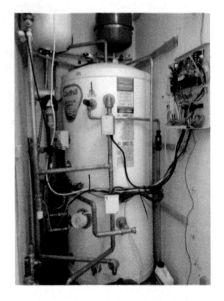

I've always admired the photography skill of installers; the bag really sets the job off.

Inside it was interesting too. No header, no buffer, no plate heat exchanger just a bypass valve, no one cared about system volume back then. No Glycol and no trvs, nowadays we call this an open system, then we called it normal.

Note how the solar coil was also used for the heat pump. Simpler times and lower cost. This is how installations are done when you are trying to keep costs down. Well before the RHI and the BUS grants.

The Samsung EHS monobloc as it was called back then, was and still is an awesome unit. It took Samsung to no 2 in the market. These machines plod on and on and on. Even at 11 years old you can still get the parts even though the unit has been upgraded 2 times since.

In conclusion:

Heat pumps are not new, they don't use any new technology, its reliable its just a fridge. They work in the same way as your freezer. and they last just as long as a boiler.

 If you don't have one you should think about it, get one in the Summer it's a good time to install one. Why wait until its cold?

Reviews:

"What's this book on?? Not more fxxking heat pumps??"

Katie Floyd, Friend, industry visionary and book critic.

Printed in Great Britain
by Amazon